A Guide for Using

The Indian in the Cupboard

in the Classroom

Based on the novel written by Lynn Reid Banks

This guide written by **Philip Denny**

Teacher Created Materials, Inc.
6421 Industry Way
Westminster, CA 92683
www.teachercreated.com
©1992 Teacher Created Materials, Inc.
Reprinted, 2000
Made in U.S.A.
ISBN-1-55734-415-9

Illustrated by
Keith Vasconcelles

Edited by
Karen J. Goldfluss, M.S. Ed.

Cover Art by
Wendy Chang

Table of Contents

Introduction

A good book can touch our lives like a good friend. Within its pages are words and characters that can inspire us to achieve our highest ideals. We can turn to it for companionship, recreation, comfort, and guidance. It also gives us a cherished story to hold in our hearts forever.

In *Literature Units,* great care has been taken to select books that are sure to become good friends!

Teachers who use this unit will find the following features to supplement their own valuable ideas.

- Sample Lesson Plans

- Pre-reading Activities

- A Biographical Sketch and Picture of the Author

- A Book Summary

- Vocabulary Lists and Suggested Vocabulary Activities

- Chapters grouped for study, with each section including:

  - *quizzes*
  - *hands-on projects*
  - *cooperative learning activities*
  - *cross-curriculum connections*
  - *extensions into the reader's own life*

- Post-reading Activities

- Book Report Ideas

- Research Ideas

- A Culminating Activity

- Three Different Options for Unit Tests

- Bibliography

- Answer Key

We are confident that this unit will be a valuable addition to your planning, and hope that as you use our ideas, your students will increase the circle of "friends" that they can have in books!

Sample Lesson Plan

Each of the lessons suggested below can take from one to several days to complete.

LESSON 1

- Introduce and complete some or all of the pre-reading activities found on page 5.
- Read "About the Author" with your students. (page 6)
- Introduce the vocabulary list for Section 1. (page 8)

LESSON 2

- Read Chapters 1-3. As you read, place the vocabulary words in the context of the story and discuss their meanings.
- Choose a vocabulary activity. (page 9)
- Build a tepee. (page 11)
- Write mottos for characters. (page 12)
- Draw a long house. (page 13)
- Begin "Reading Response Journals." (page 14)
- Administer the Section 1 quiz. (page 10)
- Introduce the vocabulary list for Section 2. (page 8)

LESSON 3

- Read Chapters 4-6. Place the vocabulary words in context and discuss their meanings.
- Choose a vocabulary activity. (page 9)
- Build a long house and write how Little Bear became lost. (page 16)
- Develop character webs and write a group play. (page 17)
- Learn about the history of the Iroquois. (page 18)
- Research the history of the bow and arrow. Make models. (page 19)
- Administer Section 2 quiz. (page 15)
- Introduce the vocabulary list for Section 3. (page 8)

LESSON 4

- Read Chapters 7-9. Place the vocabulary words in context and discuss their meanings.
- Choose a vocabulary activity. (page 9)
- Discover creative hiding places. (page 21)
- Write adventure stories in cooperative groups. (page 22)
- Make literary comparisons of characters and novels. (page 23)
- Make a list of values and support reasons for choosing each one. (page 24)

- Administer Section 3 quiz. (page 20)
- Introduce the vocabulary list for Section 4. (page 8)

LESSON 5

- Read Chapters 10-12. Place the vocabulary words in context and discuss their meanings.
- Choose a vocabulary activity. (page 9)
- Plan and prepare a breakfast. (page 26)
- Outline appropriate consequences. (page 27)
- Play Native American games. (page 28)
- Create techniques for eliminating conflicts. (page 29)
- Administer Section 4 quiz. (page 25)
- Introduce the vocabulary list for Section 5. (page 8)

LESSON 6

- Read Chapters 13-16. Place the vocabulary words in context and discuss their meanings.
- Choose a vocabulary activity. (page 9)
- Complete a missing person data sheet. (page 31)
- Make cooperative group murals of Boone's town. (page 32)
- Write and tell tall tales and legends. (page 33)
- Explore friendships. (page 34)
- Administer Section 5 quiz. (page 30)

LESSON 7

- Discuss any questions your students may have about the story. (page 35)
- Assign book reports and research projects. (pages 36 and 37)
- Begin work on culminating activity. (pages 38, 39, 40 and 41)

LESSON 8

- Administer unit tests 1,2 and/or 3. (pages 42, 43, and 44)
- Discuss the test answers and possibilities.
- Discuss the students' enjoyment of the book.
- Provide a list of related reading for your students. (page 45)

Before the Book

Before you begin reading *The Indian in the Cupboard* with your students, do some pre-reading activities to stimulate interest and enhance comprehension. Here are some activities that might work well in your class.

1. Predict what the story might be about just by hearing the title.

2. Predict what the story might be about just by looking at the cover illustration.

3. Find out if students have heard of Lynne Reid Banks, and if they know anything about her personal life or her writing.

4. Answer these questions.

   • Are you interested in:

      - stories that take place in foreign countries?

      - stories that show true friendship?

      - stories where friendships are tested?

      - stories that involve values?

      - stories that involve fantasy and adventure?

   • Would you ever:

      - believe in magic?

      - keep a secret from your own family?

      - change historical events?

      - misbehave in class?

      - create a fuss in the principal's office?

5. Have you ever kept a secret even though you knew that you might get in trouble for doing so? Explain what the secret was and what happened in detail.

6. Work in groups or as a class to create your own fantasy story.

7. Use the picture on page 48 to help introduce *The Indian in the Cupboard* to your class. The picture can also be used as a journal cover or the centerpiece of a bulletin board display of student work.

About the Author

Lynne Reid Banks was born in London, England on July 31, 1929, to Dr. James and Muriel Reid Banks. She acknowledges that she "was the only child of highly contrasted and interesting parents." Her father was a Scottish doctor born in India. Her mother was a gifted actress who was once a star on the London stage. In her earlier years, Lynne was only interested in two subjects: English and drama.

Just before World War II, Lynne Reid Banks went to a Catholic convent situated in the English countryside. The girls in her school were given a great deal of freedom. She and her friends formed their first secret society called "The League of the Deadly Nightshade." She said that "she adored secret societies," including those in which one had to "sign declarations in blood" to join, or suffer "terrifying initiations."

She went to Queen's Secretarial College from 1945-1946. In 1946, Lynne entered Italia Conte Stage School, an acting school, followed by a two year enrollment at the Royal Academy of Dramatic Arts. From 1949-1954, Lynne Reid Banks became an actress. She also worked as a journalist and a television news reporter. Lynne changed careers once again and taught high school English until 1971. Finally, she left the high school to become a professional writer.

Lynne Reid Banks lives in a large house with a huge garden in West London. The names of two of her children, Adiel and Gillon, are mentioned in *The Indian in the Cupboard*.

The author of *The Indian in the Cupboard* has mixed feelings about writing. Although she prefers writing stories for children, she writes for adults as well and has won awards in both categories. She states that writing is the hardest and loneliest work in the world. Personal satisfaction comes only with the completed piece of work. Then she adds, nothing beats "holding your own book in your own hands and looking through it and knowing that there are people all over the world reading it and perhaps...enjoying it."

(Quotations and information from *Something About the Author,* ed. by Anne Commine. Volume 22. Gale, 1980)

The Indian in the Cupboard

by Lynne Reid Banks

Avon, 1982

(Available in Canada from Avon, in U.K. from Lions and in Australia from Transworld Publishers.)

The story takes place in England. It begins innocently enough, with a boy, Omri, celebrating his birthday and opening his presents with his family. He receives many gifts, including the one he had hoped for... a skateboard complete with kryptonic wheels, and an old cupboard in which he could arrange his "treasures." However, the present with which he is least impressed becomes the focal point of the story. For when Omri places the second-hand plastic Indian, given to him by his friend Patrick, into the cupboard and locks it with his great-grandmother's old key, the cupboard and the key work a powerful magic.

When Omri goes to bed that birthday evening, the plastic Indian comes to life. He is a real person, transported from a real time in history. His name is Little Bear, the son of an Iroquois chief. Together, Omri and Little Bear develop a unique and touching relationship. Omri discovers very quickly that Little Bear is very proud, courageous, and demanding. He insists that Omri recreate a familiar and natural environment, to include wild animals for the hunt, suitable weapons, food and shelter, and a wife. Omri decides to share the magic of the cupboard with Patrick. Against Omri's wishes, Patrick brings a horse and a gun-toting cowboy named Boone to life, creating immediate conflict and some rather dangerous and exciting adventures. When Omri decides to bring his new friends to school for the day, he encounters problems with students, teachers, the headmaster, and his best friend, Patrick.

As time passes, both Patrick and Omri realize that their small men are truly real. The boys develop a growing respect and appreciation for their new friends. Boone and Little Bear develop a better understanding of each other. It becomes obvious to Patrick and Omri that as much as they would like to keep Boone and Little Bear, they cannot. The boys decide to help make their charges happy at all cost, and, with an unselfish love, return them to their time in history.

Vocabulary Lists

On this page are vocabulary lists which correspond to each sectional grouping of chapters. Vocabulary activity ideas can be found on page 9 of this book.

SECTION 1
(Chapters 1-3)

appalled	petrified
basic	quivered
buckskin	ravenously
coherent	rigid
defiant	temptation
despised	torso
episode	sarcastic
minuscule	tantalizing
minute	uncompromisingly
secondhand	unwarily

SECTION 2
(Chapters 4-6)

boulders	halter
escarpment	bridle
recklessness	knight
reluctant	keen
inspiration	dawdling
ventured	tremendous
obvious	tomahawk
orderly	enormous
long house	dawning
greenhouse	treacherous

SECTION 3
(Chapters 7-9)

compromised	spits
packet	wrenched
maize	instinctively
debated	plaid
incredulous	warily
feeble	hypnotized
chaos	dolefully
fashioned	scowled
knapsack	bowlegged
stench	swipe

SECTION 4
(Chapters 10-12)

bandolier	transaction
gingerly	raucous
grimacing	horrid
hastily	barge
plunging	relatively
outrageous	taunting
unbearable	headmaster
musingly	hysterics
apprehension	haughtily
fiendish	loomed

SECTION 5
(Chapters 13-16)

tottered	rapture
bafflement	impulse
scornfully	transfixed
rummaging	chasm
despaired	prostrate
vouch	steeley
suspicious	residence
intrigued	vulnerable
smirk	albino
sieve	petered

    8

Vocabulary Activity Ideas

You can help your students learn and retain the vocabulary in *The Indian in the Cupboard* by providing them with interesting vocabulary activities. Here are a few ideas to try.

❏ People of all ages like to make and solve puzzles. Ask your students to make their own **Crossword Puzzles** or **Wordsearch Puzzles** using the vocabulary words from the story.

❏ Challenge your students to a **Vocabulary Bee**. This is similar to a spelling bee, but in addition to spelling each word correctly, the game participants must correctly define the words as well.

❏ Play **Vocabulary Concentration**. The goal of this game is to match vocabulary words with their definitions. Divide the class into groups of 2-5 students. Have students make two sets of cards the same size and color. On one set have them write the vocabulary words. On the second set have them write the definitions. All cards are mixed together and placed face down on a table. A player picks two cards. If the pair matches the word with its definition, the player keeps the cards and takes another turn. If the cards don't match, they are returned to their places face down to the table, and another player takes a turn. Players must concentrate to remember the locations of the words and their definitions. The game continues until all matches have been made. This is an ideal activity for free exploration time.

❏ Have your students practice their writing skills by creating sentences and paragraphs in which multiple vocabulary words are used correctly. Ask them to share their **Compact Vocabulary** sentences and paragraphs with the class.

❏ Ask your students to create paragraphs which use the vocabulary words to **Present History Lessons** that relate to the time period or historical events mentioned in the story.

❏ Challenge your students to use a specific vocabulary word from the story at least **Ten Times in One Day.** They must keep a record of when, how, and why the word was used!

❏ As a group activity, have students work together to create an **Illustrated Dictionary** of the vocabulary words.

❏ Play **Twenty Clues** with the entire class. In this game, one student selects a vocabulary word and gives clues about this word, one by one, until the class can guess the word.

❏ Play **Vocabulary Charades.** In this game, vocabulary words are acted out.

You probably have many more ideas to add to this list. Try them! See if experiencing vocabulary on a personal level increases your students' vocabulary interest and retention.

Quiz

1. On the back of this paper, write a one paragraph summary of the major events in each chapter of this section. Then complete the rest of the questions on this page.

2. At first, what is Omri's reaction to the birthday present that Patrick gives him?

   _____

   _____

3. Why does Omri like the old used cupboard that his brother gives him so much?

   _____

   _____

4. To what did the key that unlocks the cupboard belong before his mother gave it to him?

   _____

   _____

5. What does Omri discover in the cupboard the morning after his birthday?

   _____

   _____

6. Why doesn't Omri share his discovery with the rest of the family?

   _____

   _____

7. When the little Indian threatens to kill Omri, why doesn't Omri laugh at the little three inch figure?

   _____

   _____

8. Why doesn't Little Bear like the tepee offered him by Omri?

   _____

   _____

9. What does Omri find out that the cupboard and key can do?

   _____

   _____

10. To which Indian tribe does Little Bear belong?

   _____

   _____

Tepee

In this section, Omri finds out that Little Bear will not sleep in the tepee, because it is only a toy. Omri finally builds him one. This is acceptable, but only on the condition that Omri bring paints so that Little Bear can paint pictures on it to make the tepee more real. Omri also decides to take the tepee to his crafts class to sew it together properly.

Originally, the word tepee was a Sioux Indian word which meant a portable dwelling place. It was composed of a framework of poles pointed together and fastened at the top with leather twine of sorts. The poles were spread out at the bottom forming a large circle. A tent of skins was then stretched tightly around the poles and fastened at the bottom with pegs or stones. These tepees were up to 15' (4.5 m) in height and 30' (9 m) in diameter. They were used primarily by the Plains Indians as they hunted bison across the plains.

Develop symbols of animals that you might use to decorate a tepee similar to Little Bear's. Draw these symbols in the four boxes provided. Under each of your symbols, write a short caption which tells what it represents.

Now use your creative skills and, like Omri, construct a tepee approximately 10" (25 cm) in height and 5" (13 cm) in diameter. Stretch your simulated skins around the frame and fasten it down with little pegs. Place the tepee on a flat board or cardboard painted with natural earth colors. On the tepee, paint (with bright colors) the symbols which you created earlier. Explain your tepee, building materials, and symbols to the class.

More Than Just Words

A principle is a truth or law which serves as the foundation for others. It is a rule of conduct. If a person is principled, he or she shows a strong belief in integrity and honesty, and lives by certain rules of conduct. We are often judged by how well we live up to our principles.

Words or phrases, called mottos, are sometimes used to describe a principle by which a person lives. Here are some examples you may have heard. Think about the principle behind each.

> *"To thine own self be true."*
>
> *"Haste makes waste."*
>
> *"Do not judge a person until you have walked a mile in his moccasins."*
>
> *"Never pass by the chance to do a kindness, for you may never pass the same way again."*

With a partner, brainstorm possible mottos that would be appropriate for Omri and Little Bear. Consider their strongest attributes or qualities. Write a motto inside the shield for each character. Color or decorate the shields. Then, discuss with your partner a motto that would best describe a principle by which you live. You may use a familiar motto, or create a new one. Do the same for your partner. Add the mottos to the shields; color or decorate each.

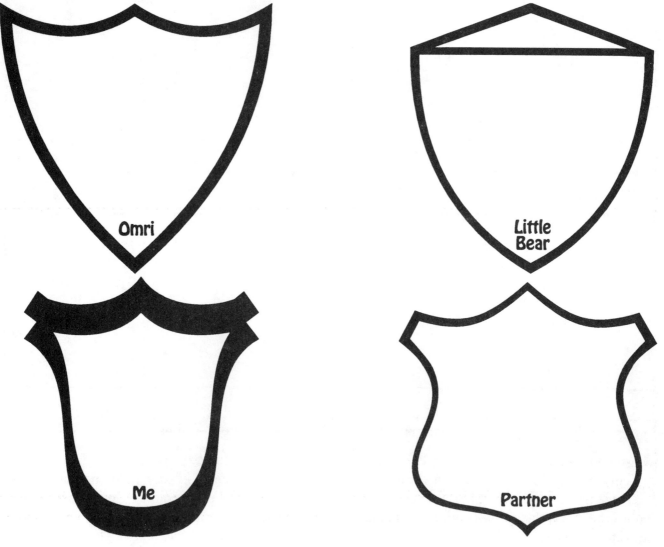

Shelter

In this section, it has been pointed out by Little Bear that the tepee was not the type of shelter used by the Iroquois Nation. His people did not migrate as did the Plains Indians. As a result, he had lived in a more permanent type of structure called a long house.

For this activity you and a partner will research how these structures were built and what types of interiors they had. Include how many people lived in each one and how the village was organized with these long houses as the central feature.

In the space provided below, you and your partner are to draw a detailed long house. In box A , show the external view of a completed long house, labelling the significant details. In box B, show the internal details or floor plan of the same long house, using factual information to create a realistic illustration. Label the fireplace, sleeping mats, and any other significant details which would be included in a traditional long house.

A

B

Note: The research and illustration from this page will be used as references for the long house activity on page 16.

Reading Response Journals

One great way to insure that the reading of *The Indian in the Cupboard* touches each student in a personal way is to include the use of Reading Response Journals in your plans. In these journals, students can be encouraged to respond to the story in a number of ways. Here are a few ideas.

- Ask students to create a journal for *The Indian in the Cupboard.* Tell students that the purpose of the journal is to record their thoughts, ideas, observations, and questions as they read *The Indian in the Cupboard.*

- Provide students with, or ask them to suggest, topics from the story that will stimulate writing. Here are a few examples from the chapters in Section 1.

  - Describe the feelings and thoughts that must have raced through his mind when Omri first saw the live Indian crouching in the darkest corner of the cupboard.

  - What do you suppose Little Bear's thoughts were when he was transported through time to find himself in a giant's cupboard?

- After reading each chapter, students can write one or more new things they learned in the chapter. Ask students to draw their responses to certain events or characters in the story, using the blank pages in their journals.

- Tell students that they may use their journals to record "diary-type" responses that they may want to enter. Encourage students to bring their journal ideas to life! Ideas generated from their journal writing can be used to create plays, debates, stories, songs, and art displays.

Allow students time to write in their journals daily. Explain to the students that their Reading Response Journals can be evaluated in a number of ways. Here are a few ideas.

- Personal reflections will be read by the teacher, but no corrections or letter grades will be assigned. Credit is given for effort, and all students who sincerely try will be awarded credit. If a grade is desired for this type of entry, grade according to the number of journal entries completed. For example, if five journal assignments were made and the student conscientiously completes all five, then he or she should receive an "A."

- Non-judgmental teacher responses should be made as you read the journals to let the students know that you are reading and enjoying their journals. Here are some types of responses that will please your journal writers and encourage them to write more.

  - "You have really found what's important in the story!"
  - "You write so clearly, I almost feel as if I am there!"
  - "If you feel comfortable doing so, I'd like you to share your idea with the class. They will enjoy what you've written!"

Quiz

1. On the back of this paper, write a one paragraph summary of the major events in each chapter of this section. Then complete the rest of the questions on this page.

2. How does Little Bear injure his leg while he is being carried by Omri?

   _____

   _____

3. Who does Omri find to administer first aid to Little Bear?

   _____

   _____

4. Why does this helper want to go back to where he came from?

   _____

   _____

5. What tool does Omri give to Little Bear so that he can work on his project?

   _____

   _____

6. What does Little Bear build while Omri is in school?

   _____

   _____

7. While doing research on the Iroquois, what does Omri learn about the practice of scalping?

   _____

   _____

8. Why does Omri rush off to Yapp's at lunchtime?

   _____

   _____

9. What does Omri make for Little Bear during handicrafts class?

   _____

   _____

10. What happens to the Chief when Omri performs magic and brings him to life?

    _____

    _____

The Long House

The following activities are extensions of the research you and your partners did in the last section on long houses. Discuss and list as a class the results of each group's research on long houses. Use the accumulated, accurate information gathered to complete the activities below.

On page 13, you found out how these communal dwellings were constructed. The Iroquois first constructed a long house framed with poles. Over this frame they shingled a skin on by sewing pieces of bark to the top and sides of the house. A long hall stretched end to end with areas sectioned off on either side for the sleeping area.

Activity 1: You and your partner are to build a long house with a floor plan and structure similar to the drawings you made on page 13. Use as many items from nature as possible in your long house construction. The platform beds and shelves could be wooden and tied together with twine or similar natural substances. The fire pits down the hallway might be lined with pebbles or small rocks. Use your own imagination, but try to utilize the natural elements as the Iroquois would have done.

Your long house should be no longer than two feet (.6 m), but large enough to have an interior with sleeping quarters and some scattered artifacts (bow and arrow, etc.) in the family areas.

Long House Model

Activity 2: Brainstorm with your partner to create a dialogue between Little Bear's father and five others discussing what might have happened to his son. How did he vanish? Was he captured by the Algonquins or the French?

After reaching a common consensus have the chief decide on what action to take. This dialogue should take place in the long house at the communal fireplace between the rooms. Write your final copy in ink and attach it to the bottom of your completed long house.

Present your dialogue to the class and show them your long house. Add models to represent the characters in your dialogue. Display completed long houses and dialogues at an appropriate school location.

When Characters Come to Life

In this section Omri introduces more of his plastic toys to the magic of his cupboard. He can make any plastic toy come to life. A World War I medic, Tommy Atkins tends to Little Bear's injured leg. An old chief comes to life for a brief moment and Little Bear is able to borrow his cloak, headdress, and the chief's bow and arrows. The cupboard is a time machine which transports the figures molded in plastic out of a real time period and specific place, into the present.

Imagine that other characters have come to life in the cupboard and are now together in Omri's room. What do you think would happen? What might the characters say to each other? Who might become friends?

Working in a group of four, consider the personality traits and physical appearances of the following characters: Little Bear; the old Indian chief; Tommy; the knight. Have each member of your group choose one of the characters and develop it in such a way that the character becomes as real as possible. Use information given in the book as well as your own imagination.

First, develop the traits of a character you have chosen by making a character web. Use the following directions and the sample web below to help you better understand your character. Then make a web on a separate paper and fill in each section with the appropriate information about your chosen character.

- Write the name of the character (or draw a picture) in the center circle.
- Write specific character traits (proud, mean, lazy, selfish, considerate, etc.) for your character in the boxes.
- In the ovals radiating from the boxes, give examples of events from the story to support the trait.

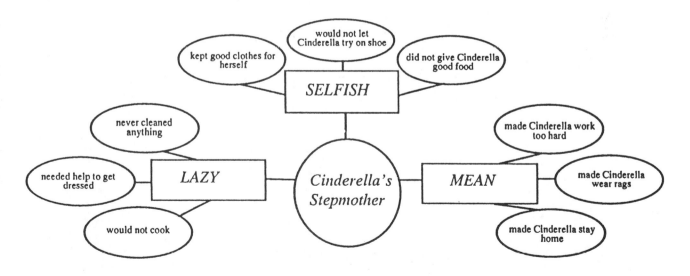

Now that the characters have been developed by each group member, they will interact in a group play. Some possibilities for your play might be:

   Tommy is injured during the war and Little Bear administers aid to him.

   Little Bear saves the knight's life. The knight rewards him.

   The old Indian chief does not die, but is too ill to remain as chief.

History and Geography

Little Bear is the son of an Iroquois chief. The Iroquois Nation was formed in the 1400s in what is today called the Finger Lakes Region of New York state. Five tribes, the Cayuga, Seneca, Mohawk, Oneida, and Onondaga, formed a Confederation, or group of societies that came together to work cooperatively toward the common goals of peace and survival. By the 1500s, the Confederation of Five Nations became very powerful and controlled territory from New York to the Mississippi.

Native American history is rich in culture, tradition, and legacy. It is estimated that today, about 50,000 Iroquois are citizens of the United States or Canada. Learn more about the Iroquois Nation by researching and sharing information you discover about the Iroquois tribes.

Choose from among the following topics, or expand your research into an area of interest you may develop as you study the Iroquois Nation:

- The Council of 49
- The Legend of Hiawatha
- The Tuscarora Indians
- The Iroquoian language

- Fur trade among the Iroquois
- The Iroquois role in the French and Indian War
- The role of the Iroquois League in the American Revolution

When you have completed your report, present it to the class. Provide a visual display, such as a map, pictures, charts, or overhead transparencies to add more interest to your information.

Below is a partial map of New York state. For the following activity you will locate the five original members of the Iroquois Nation in the 1500s as well as certain map features. Consult an atlas or similar reference source to help you fill in the significant geographic landmarks that are necessary to effectively chart the area ruled by this powerful league. The boundaries of each league member's area have been provided. Lightly color each section and label the tribe that controlled that area. Include a map key and symbol guide for easy reference. Be sure to identify the lakes, rivers, and mountains.

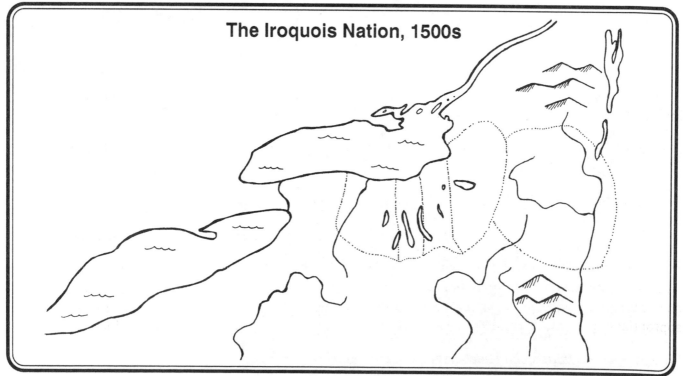

The Iroquois Nation, 1500s

Bows and Arrows

In this section Omri grants Little Bear's request for a bow and arrows. Little Bear realizes that it is dangerous in this new world and a brave must have his tools and weapons. Now that he is the new chief, he has increased his demands and wants Omri to produce deer so he can hunt for his own food.

Bows and arrows have been used for approximately 3,000 years. Assyrian archers of 700 BC used heavy bows and arrows in their conquests. The Persian empire replaced the Assyrian bow design by making shorter bows which they wielded with accuracy while on horseback.

The best known bow is the Welsh or English Long Bow. This formidable weapon was 6 feet (1.8 m) in height and could easily fire heavy arrows 600 feet (180 m) in the air with deadly accuracy. It changed the tactics of warfare in Europe. Fletchings were added to the ends of the arrow shaft to give directional stability during flight. These stabilizers were made out of feathers, hair, or thin strips of wood. The arrow tips changed according to usage.

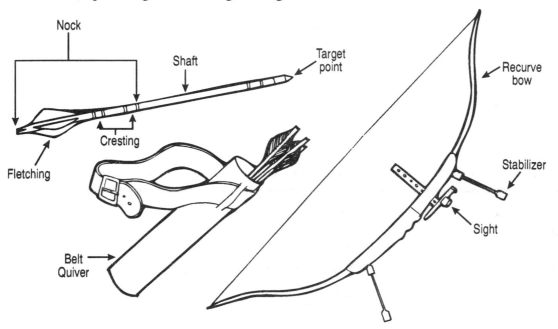

Find out more about these time-honored weapons by researching the history of the bow and arrow. Include the following in your report:

- Explain some of the different types of bows, pointing out their advantages and disadvantages from ancient times to the present.

- Illustrate and label one of the bows you have chosen to write about.

- Discuss some of the various types of arrows and the uses of different arrow tips. Illustrate and label one of the arrows you have chosen to write about.

After you have finished your research paper, make a model bow and arrow. It should be modeled after one of the types discussed in your research paper. Remember to decorate your bow and arrows appropriately with the type of symbols or materials commonly used during the time period.

Present your findings to the class and show your model.

Quiz

1. On the back of this paper, write a one paragraph summary of the major events that happen in each of the chapters of this section. Then complete the rest of the questions on this page.

2. What does Omri buy for his father at the hardware store?

_____

_____

3. What new present does Patrick buy for Omri?

_____

_____

4. What is Patrick's great idea for keeping Little Bear's fire burning longer?

_____

_____

5. While Omri is getting some stew for Little Bear, what is Patrick doing in Omri's room?

_____

_____

6. Why does Omri agree to bring the cowboy and Little Bear to school the next day?

_____

_____

7. How do the cowboy and his horse get out of the dressing-up crate?

_____

_____

8. Why does Boone think that this is all a " 'gol darned hallucy-nation?' "

_____

_____

9. When and why does Little Bear promise that he will do a dance for Omri?

_____

_____

10. What name do Boone's friends give him and why?

_____

_____

Hiding Places

Omri hid his long house and seed tray behind his dressing-up crate. However, this precaution didn't seem to stop his brother from snooping about and finding the long house. To hide something successfully takes careful planning. You might need to consider the size, shape, texture, or accessibility of the item into or onto which you plan to disguise or hide the object. For example, a diary could be placed inside a hollowed out book that is seldom read.

Brainstorm with the class things that they have hidden and where or what the secret hiding places were. These ideas should generate further suggestions as to where they could hide something as big as the seed tray or the long house.

For this activity, create what you consider to be the perfect hiding place for some of the following: a long house; a horse; Little Bear; a tepee; bow and arrows.

In the box below, draw a sketch of a bedroom and include IN PLAIN VIEW the source of your hiding place for the above items. On the back of the paper, tell where you hid the objects and how your hiding place works. (For instance, maybe you used an old trunk for a lamp table. The long house could fit inside the trunk.)

When you have finished, ask other students to look at the picture and make guesses as to where the hiding places are.

It's a Small World

In this section Omri builds a fire at night just before bedtime in order for Little Bear to relax in front of his long house.

> *"Omri turned off his light and drew back from the scene. It looked amazingly real, with the fire making shadows, the little horse munching his grain, and the Indian sitting on his heels warming himself, wearing his colorful headdress and chief's cloak. Omri wished he himself were small enough to join Little Bear by the fire."*

You may recall the way in which Omri began to see things as he observed Little Bear's encounter with his new surroundings. Little stones became boulders, weeds became trees, and ants made Little Bear's horse shy.

Imagine, as Omri did, what it would be like to be the size of Little Bear. Work with a partner or two and create an adventure in which you are magically transformed in size, and join Little Bear at his camp. Remember that the events take place at night and you are in Omri's room. If you go outside, you must include a description of how you get down the stairs and out the door. What kind of scary night creatures will be out there to greet you? How will you protect yourself? Try to use everyday items in this adventure: a button for a shield, or a broken pin for a sword. Your short dream should include how you join up with Little Bear, the problems that you encounter and how you overcome these obstacles, and the way in which you return to your real self.

Use the boxes below to brainstorm a list of everyday items that may be used or seen as something quite different when you are very small. Write your adventure on separate paper or in your journal. Sketch a picture of you and Little Bear in action.

Real Item

_____

_____

_____

_____

_____

b e c o m e s

In My Small World

_____

_____

_____

_____

_____

Comparing Literature

Often stories have similar plots or themes. The characters may have common personalities or physical appearances. The events may follow a similar path. There is a story that is similar to *The Indian in the Cupboard*. In *The Castle in the Attic*, by Elizabeth Winthrop, Mrs. Phillips gives ten year old Lawrence a castle as a going away present. With the castle comes a tiny silver knight that comes to life by William's touch. William discovers that this knight is not a toy, but a true knight who had been transformed by an evil wizard's magic. The knight that William brings to life has a rich and full past, just as Omri's Little Bear does.

Read *The Castle in the Attic* independently, or as a class and make comparisons between the main characters and the story plot in the two novels. Think about the following questions as you make the comparisons:

- How do the living conditions and the personalities of Omri and William compare?
- Both boys have best friends. How does the involvement of the best friends compare in the two novels?
- Do Little Bear and Sir Simon come to life in similar ways?
- How are Little Bear and Sir Simon alike and different?
- How do the boys compare when it comes to keeping their magical worlds secret?
- How active a role does each boy play in the adventures of his miniature character?
- How does each story introduce the miniature characters?

The diagram below is called a Venn diagram. Use the ideas generated from the questions above to compare either Omri and William, or Little Bear and Sir Simon. In the outside section of the circles, write some of the ways in which the two characters are different. The inner section, where the circles overlap, is to be used for writing similarities between the characters.

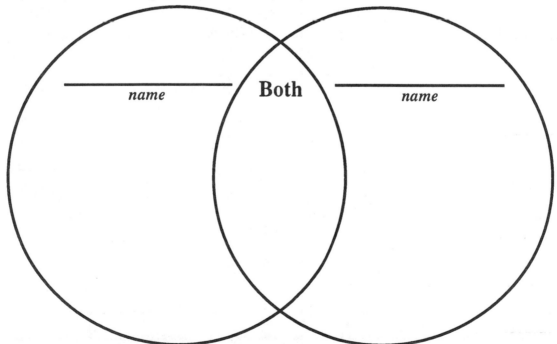

When you have finished reading *The Indian in the Cupboard*, compare the adventures and problems in each novel and make a Venn diagram to show how they are alike and different.

Values

The Iroquois have great reverence toward the land. They believe that plants and animals have their own spirits and call upon those spirits for help in farming and hunting. They value and respect the land, taking only what they need and nothing more. They work together and share with each other in times of need.

A value is the worth or quality of a thing that makes it useful, important, or desirable. Values are strong beliefs or standards by which one lives. Little Bear demonstrates a sense of values through his words and deeds. As a brave he finds it important to hunt for his own food and to use only what is necessary from the environment. When Omri tells Little Bear that he will be given food whenever he needs it, Little Bear becomes upset and replies, "Little Bear chief now. Chief hunts. Kills own meat. Not take meat others kill. If not hunt, lose skill with bow." Pride in doing a job well and with great skill are important to the young chief. Omri values friendship and is responsible and sensitive as well. Several times he reminds Patrick not to abuse life. He will not let Patrick make Boone real, because Boone and Little Bear would fight. He is clearly concerned that they might hurt each other. Despite the fact that Patrick ignores Omri's warning and brings Boone to life, Omri forgives him and shares his secret because they are friends and "that counts for a lot in this life."

Have you ever taken the time to assess what is really important in your life? For some people, material things, such as clothes, toys, or a fancy skateboard are important. What values are important in your life? Which values are more important? What about people who are valued by you? Do you have good friends? What qualities do you look for in a friend?

Have your class brainstorm and list ideas that they value in life. From this list compile the five most important items in each of the following categories and list them in order of importance (the most important one first and the least important last) in the chart below.

Important Things	*Important People*	*Important Values*
_____	_____	_____
_____	_____	_____
_____	_____	_____
_____	_____	_____
_____	_____	_____

Choose one of the categories and write a paragraph discussing why you selected the items and why you rated them the way that you did. Share your selections with the class.

Quiz

1. On the back of this paper, write a one paragraph summary of the major events in each chapter of this section. Then complete the rest of the questions of this page.

2. Why does Little Bear scornfully call Omri a woman?

    _____

    _____

3. What is the condition that Omri makes with Little Bear and Boone before they can eat their breakfasts?

    _____

    _____

4. What happens immediately after breakfast?

    _____

    _____

5. How does the cowboy respond when Omri suggests that he wash his clothes?

    _____

    _____

6. What situation does Omri tell Little Bear and Boone might occur if they get taken away from him?

    _____

    _____

7. Why do Patrick and Omri get kicked out of the main hall?

    _____

    _____

8. What happens to Patrick during lunch that has Omri's heart "hammering with terror?"

    _____

    _____

9. Why does Omri regret giving the two men to Patrick?

    _____

    _____

10. When Patrick leaves the headmaster's office, why is the headmaster's face "dead white?"

    _____

    _____

Breakfast

Have you ever tried to prepare a meal for yourself or other family members? Although we are told that Omri was quite a good cook, there is room for doubt. When he tried to cook beans and an egg for his guests, he broke the egg and the crumbled egg shells into the pan together on the hot fat. When some of the beans got into the egg pan they "seemed to explode." Finally, with the egg's center still uncooked, and while the beans in the pan were still "stone cold" Omri dumped the whole mess into a bowl. Breakfast, such as it was, was ready!

Here is an opportunity to give others the recipe for your favorite breakfast food. Fill in the recipe card below. Then, try the activity at the bottom of the page.

Breakfast Food

Cooking utensils needed:

_____

_____

_____

_____

picture

Ingredients:

_____

_____

Directions:

_____

_____

_____

_____

_____

Next, bring in the necessary items and act as though you were a cooking instructor on TV. Using your "props," hold up the items and go through your instructions from start to finish on how to prepare your fantastic breakfast. If possible, share your creation with the audience when you are finished.

Facing the Consequences

Patrick and Omri demonstrated inappropriate behavior in the following situations. Because their actions were disruptive or in some way broke the school rules of conduct, they must accept the consequences.

As you analyze each situation in small groups, consider both sides of each issue, and choose an appropriate consequence for their misconduct. Write your collective thoughts on the lines provided.

Situation 1: At lunch, "Omri slammed his empty tray on the floor," and yanked Patrick out of the lunch line.

_____

_____

_____

_____

Situation 2: Patrick skipped class and lied to the teacher.

_____

_____

_____

_____

Situation 3: Both boys continued to cause trouble and were kicked out of class.

_____

_____

_____

_____

Situation 4: Omri knocked Patrick to the floor in the headmaster's office and threatened to kill Patrick; then, kicked and banged the door with his fists.

_____

_____

_____

_____

Native American Games

What kinds of games do you think Little Bear might have played in his own time? In addition to having fun, the games we play often improve our agility and endurance. Many of the games enjoyed by Native American children are both fun and purposeful. Try some of the following Native American kicking and throwing games.

Kickball Races

These races were very popular especially with Southwestern tribes. They varied in length from 1 to 25 miles. The balls ranged from 2 ¹/₂" (6 cm) to 4 ¹/₂" (11 cm) in diameter. They were made of many different materials depending on what was available in the tribe's region. The Pueblo People often stuffed the balls with the hair from fast animals—the horse, the rabbit, and hair from the big toe of a fast runner from the tribe!

The ball for this activity may be a softball or you may make your own. Start with a 1" (2.5 cm) to 1 ¹/₂" (4 cm) diameter rock, add hair from a fast animal if desired, cover with newspaper, and wrap with masking tape. Designate someone to be chief. As chief, he or she will design the race. Native Americans ran this race over all types of terrain. They were never allowed to touch the ball with their hands—even if it landed in a river! Have races with your friends. Plot a course for your race. Line up at a starting point and have each player kick his or her ball to a finish line.

Kick Stick Race

This was a popular and strenuous game played by Native Americans. It was played the same way as kickball (above), but used a stick instead. The stick varied from 2 ¹/₂" (6 cm) to 10" (25 cm) long and ³/₄" (2 cm) to 1 ¹/₂" (4 cm) in diameter. A 1" dowel cut about 5" (13 cm) long will work very well for this game.

The Zuni believed that the stick contained magic that drew the runner along. Each stick was decorated and an owner would never part with a successful stick.

Have fun racing from a start to a finish line while kicking a stick similar to the Zuni stick.

Toss Ball Game

This is a very simple game to play. You will need an old tennis ball that has lost its bounce, or a softball. Draw a straight line in the dirt with a stick. Each player in turn must place him or herself flat on his or her back, with shoulders on this line. Place the ball in the palm of the hand and outstretch the arm above the head, touching the ground. The player then throws the ball as far as possible. (You may be surprised at the results!) The spot where the ball lands is marked with a stone. The player who throws the ball the farthest is the winner.

Trouble-Shooters

Several fights and disputes erupted throughout the story; some between Patrick and Omri, others between Little Bear and Boone. Have you ever been in a fight? Was it physical or verbal? On the back of this paper, describe the situation that caused this conflict. If not, recall a conflict that someone you know has experienced, or one you may have read about in a favorite book.

Avoiding conflict is not always easy. However, there are ways to handle potentially explosive situations effectively. Below are some ideas on how to trouble-shoot conflicts. After discussing these trouble-shooters, apply them to the activity at the bottom of the page.

- **Apologize.** It sounds simple, but is often all the other party needs to hear. Sometimes an explanation of why you are sorry will help, too.

- **Take time out.** Take a few seconds to think before you respond to an action or insult. Think of different options available to you and their consequences. Take the action that is best for both of you.

- **Take turns telling each side of the problem.** Let the other person go first and be sure he or she has had an opportunity to express his or her feelings. Then take your turn. Tell the other person that you are upset with him or her and why. Maybe this person is unaware that he or she is the cause of your anger.

- **Teachers, parents, or other people you both respect** are good sources to help mediate the problem. If you mutually solve it you both win.

- **Make a joke of the situation.** This releases tension and again results in a win/win situation. It defuses problems.

- **Simply walk away.** This is sometimes hard to do, especially if other people are watching to see what you will do. However, it takes a lot of courage to do so, and you gain respect as well as avoid further conflict.

- **The best way to avoid conflict is to stay out of trouble in the first place.** Be aware of how your actions might look to others. Be sensitive enough not to hurt people's feelings or embarrass them.

Activity:

Rewrite a fight scene from the story using one of the above methods or one of your own to solve the conflict. Add dialogue between characters in your rewriting of the scene.

Quiz

1. On the back of this paper, write a one paragraph summary of the major events in each chapter of this section. Then complete the rest of the questions of this page.

2. Why does Patrick tell the headmaster about the little men?

    _____

    _____

3. What is Omri's reason for prohibiting Patrick from keeping the cowboy?

    _____

    _____

4. What new demand does Little Bear make to Omri that threatens to turn his fun into a nightmare?

    _____

    _____

5. What talent does Omri discover about Boone that delights him?

    _____

    _____

6. What does Patrick do to help patch up his fight with Omri?

    _____

    _____

7. Why do Little Bear and Boone exchange frightened looks when Omri announces that the magic is gone?

    _____

    _____

8. What happens to Boone while he is watching the cowboy and Indian movie on television?

    _____

    _____

9. Who finds the key?

    _____

    _____

10. Why do the boys decide to leave the cupboard empty at the end of the story?

    _____

    _____

Have You Seen . . .?

Little Bear and Boone have been missing from their time. Imagine that you are living in the time and place from which Boone or Little Bear came. Use the facts from the story and what you know about one of these characters to complete the following data sheet.

Missing Person Data Sheet

Missing Person: _____

Person filing report: _____

Date last seen: _____

Place last seen: _____

_____

Last seen wearing: _____

(picture)

_____

_____

Last seen doing: _____

_____

_____

Place most likely to be found: _____

_____

Things most likely to be doing: _____

_____

_____

If found, please notify: _____

_____

Picture This!

Boone did not seem to play the role of a cowboy very well. Perhaps he was in the wrong profession. As he told Omri, " 'Art, eh? Say, that waz mah best subject!' " He proceeded to draw his hometown. His drawing was set in a prairie landscape, with hills, cacti, and a bit of sagebrush. He sketched in a wooden building of the type Omri used to see in cowboy movies. He drew a saloon with a swinging sign reading "Golden Dollar Saloon." Among the other details of Boone's picture were: a general store, a livery stable, and a stone house with barred windows (the jail). In the street scene, he included "men and women, wagons, horses, dogs, and all the trappings of a little town."

Work in cooperative groups of three or four people. Using a piece of white or light colored butcher paper about 6 feet (2 meters) long, create a mural-type drawing similar to the picture that Boone sketched. You might want to use charcoal or colored chalk as your medium. Try to include as many items as Boone drew. Divide the items to be used in the sketch among group members. Use the rest of this page as a sketch pad, and practice drawing those objects for which you are responsible. When the group is ready, decide where each of the group's sketches will be placed on the butcher paper and begin your group mural. Display your murals.

Tell Me a Story

Two popular forms of storytelling are the tall tale and the legend. Since the beginning of time, the art of storytelling has been a way of keeping the past alive. Before written language, there were the fire circles where a clan's history would be recounted. Often storytelling served as an instructional tool as well as a form of entertainment. In the Middle Ages, the exploits of knights were told and retold in the great halls of the lords as forms of entertainment for the masses and to glorify the knights.

The Tall Tale

This time honored art was very much in existence in the new world as well. The skill evolved in the west into what is known as the tall tale. A tall tale is a story based on fact, but told in a highly exaggerated and humorous way. The deeds of the hero or heroine sometimes border on the ridiculous. The story of Rip Van Winkle is an example of this kind of tale.

Activity:

Write and share your own tall tale. Imagine that you are listening in at Boone's favorite saloon, The Golden Dollar. A few customers are telling a tenderfoot the story of Boohoo Boone, who "tied one on" and rode out of town never to be seen again. Include and exaggerate some of Boone's character traits, and create a magical tale of what finally happened to make him vanish off the face of the earth! Naturally, they are pulling the tenderfoot's leg, so do your best to s-t-r-e-t-c-h the truth.

The Legend

A legend is a type of folk story. Most legends have as their subjects recognizable people, events, or places. While some are based on real persons or events, many revolve around imaginary characters, some of which have extraordinary powers. Pecos Bill and Paul Bunyan are examples. Most societies or cultures have local and national legends. These usually reinforce the ideals or attitudes of the people. Such legends emphasize those qualities that the people most admire.

The legend of Hiawatha is well known among the members of the Iroquois Nation. In this legend, the Mohawk chief, Hiawatha, met with the god Dekanawida (dee kahn uh WEE duh) to help bring peace to the tribes and unite them into a single Iroquois Nation. Although it has not been proven that Hiawatha lived, his legendary words were treasured by the Iroquois. In the 1400s, the tribes united and formed a Great Council of 49 chiefs.

Activity:

Create and tell a legend of your own around the character, Little Bear. In this legend, focus on qualities such as bravery and determination (perhaps in a battle against the Algonquin or the French). Introduce an element of magic at the end of the story. (For example, you could relate that Little Bear is now among the stars and that his people await his return.)

The Indian in the Cupboard

Friendships

Despite moments when Patrick and Omri had strong disagreements and actual fights, they remained good friends. Patrick gave Little Bear and Boone to Omri. He had a good suggestion about how to bring fire to Little Bear and he stood by Omri at Mr. Yapp's when Omri was accused of stealing.

Omri demonstrated his friendship and loyalty to Patrick on several occasions as well. He went against his own instincts and let Patrick in on the secret of the Indian in the cupboard. He allowed Patrick to keep the cowboy even though he had misgivings.

Concessions and compromises are sometimes necessary in a friendship. In small groups, or as a class, discuss the following questions about friendship.

- What qualities do you look for in a friend?

- Have you ever had any fights or disagreements with your friends? What were they about? How did you resolve them?

Now, write and send the following note to a good friend. Let your friend know that you are thinking about him or her. Perhaps you could thank your friend for being helpful, thoughtful, etc.

_____
(date)

Dear_____,

_____

_____

_____

_____

_____

Your friend,

_____

Any Questions?

When you finished reading *The Indian in the Cupboard*, did you have some questions that were left unanswered? Write your questions here.

_____

_____

_____

_____

Work alone or in groups to prepare possible answers for the questions you asked above and those written below. When you finish your predictions, share your ideas with the class.

- Did Omri's mother know that the key was magic?
- Did the key perform magic on the old jewelry box, too?
- Why didn't Little Bear ask where he was right away?
- Why didn't Omri take Little Bear for a tour of his room?
- Did Little Bear ever tell Omri of any specific battles against the French? Where did these battles take place? Could Little Bear even tell who was winning the war?
- How did Little Bear raise the big beams of the long house by himself?
- How did Little Bear calm the Arabian horse so easily?
- How did Little Bear know about horses since he said he walked everywhere?
- What do you think Tommy told his fellow soldiers from World War I about his disappearance? Did he get into any trouble?
- When did Omri first become sensitive to the fact that Little Bear was a real human with a life of his own?
- Didn't Omri ever feel guilty about keeping Little Bear prisoner?
- After the trouble between Little Bear and Boone began that first morning, why didn't Omri just send Boone back?
- Why didn't the lunch lady discipline the boys?
- Why didn't the headmaster discipline Omri and Patrick when he kicked them out of the assembly?
- Why didn't Omri clean up the mess in the kitchen, since he was so concerned about not letting his parents know he was cooking?
- How did Little Bear know that white men were stealing Indian lands?
- Do you think the headmaster ever told his secretary what happened?
- What do you think the headmaster did after he had time to think about the incident?
- Was the teacher mad that the headmaster did nothing to the boys?
- What happened when Little Bear and Boone returned home?

Book Report Ideas

There are numerous ways to do a book report. After you have finished reading *The Indian in the Cupboard*, choose one method of reporting that interests you. It may be a way that your teacher suggests, an idea of your own or one of the ways mentioned below.

- **See What I Read?**

This report is a visual one. A model of a scene from the story can be created, or a likeness of one or more of the characters from the story can be drawn or sculpted.

- **Time Capsule**

This report provides people living at a "future" time with the reasons *The Indian in the Cupboard* is such an outstanding book, and gives these "future" people reasons why it should be read. Make a time capsule type of design, and neatly print or write your reasons inside the capsule. You may wish to bury your capsule after you have shared it with your classmates. Perhaps one day someone will find it and read *The Indian in the Cupboard* because of what you wrote.

- **The Perfect Gift**

For this report, you will be responsible for choosing a different and appropriate gift for three of the characters from *The Indian in the Cupboard*. Your gifts must be selected from the items you have available to you. Describe or draw a picture of each gift, name the person it will be given to, and explain why it is the perfect gift for him or her.

- **Guess Who or What!**

This report takes the form of several games of "Twenty Questions." The reporter gives a series of general to specific clues about a character from the story, and students guess the identity of the mystery character. After the character has been identified, the same reporter presents another "Twenty Questions" about an event in the story.

- **A Character Comes to Life!**

Suppose one of the characters in *The Indian in the Cupboard* came to life and walked into your home or classroom. This report describes what this character sees, hears, and feels as he or she experiences the world in which you live.

- **Sales Talk**

This report serves as an advertisement to "sell" *The Indian in the Cupboard*. You decide which group to target and the sales pitch you will use. Include graphics in your presentation.

- **Coming Attraction!**

The Indian in the Cupboard is about to be made into a movie and you have been chosen to design the promotional poster. Include the title and author of the book, a listing of the main characters and the contemporary actors who will play them, a drawing of a scene from the book, and a paragraph synopsis of the story.

- **Literary Interview**

This report is done in pairs. One student pretends to be a character in the story. The other student will play the role of a television or radio interviewer, providing the audience with insights into the character's personality and life. It is the responsibility of the partners to create meaningful questions and appropriate responses.

Research Ideas

Describe three things you read in *The Indian in the Cupboard* that you want to learn more about.

1. _____

2. _____

3. _____

As you read *The Indian in the Cupboard*, you encountered geographical locations, historical events, culturally diverse people, and prejudices. To increase your understanding of the characters and events in the story as well as more fully recognize Lynne Reid Banks' craft as a writer, research to find out more about these people, places and things!

Work in groups to research one or more of the areas you named above, or the areas that are mentioned below. Share your findings with the rest of the class in any appropriate form of oral presentation.

The French and Indian War
- The causes
- The expansion to North America
- The geographic regions involved
- Native American, French, and British involvement
- Famous French and English officers
- Significant Battles
- Types of weaponry
- Outcome of the war

American West in 1800's
- Settlements
- Native Americans in western regions
- Cowboys' lifestyle and famous names
- U.S. Cavalry

The Iroquois Nation
- members of
- geographical area
- tribal beliefs
- arts/crafts
- religion
- famous leaders
- weapons of war
- enemies
- relationships with settlers
- myths and legends

Diorama

In this culminating activity, you will be working with no more than three partners in a cooperative learning experience. You will be creating a diorama of one of the scenes from *The Indian in the Cupboard.*

As a group, choose an appropriate scene for your diorama. Some ideas would be: Little Bear and his first outside ride with his new horse; the scene with Little Bear stalking the cowboy on their first meeting; the breakfast scene; or, the first meeting of Bright Stars and Little Bear.

Organize yourselves according to skill strengths and decide which part of this project each of you could do best. (For example, which member has artistic ability and shows interest in drawing the background that would be necessary? Who would work well with wood tools, or who has the ability to work with clay to fashion the figures, etc?)

Decide the steps that will be ideal for the successful completion of your representation. What must be done first, second, third, fourth, and so on?

You will need a sturdy box to house your particular scene. Be sure that its size meets your needs. Gather and assemble all of your materials in a central location.

Draw a picture for the back of the diorama which will be the setting for your scene.

Create the figures you are going to use by hand. These could be made from wood, clay or any other medium that is available to you.

If you include a tepee or long house, try to use natural materials as did Little Bear. If it is an outdoor scene, include shrubs, dirt, pebbles, sticks with leaves glued on; anything to make it as realistic as possible. Include as many details and be as creative as possible in designing your 3-dimensional reproduction of a scene from the book.

Dramatizing the Diorama

This activity is an extension of the diorama which you and your team just completed. You will need a blank cassette tape and a tape recorder in order to create an audio dramatization to go along with your diorama.

This recording can be presented with the different members of your team narrating a summary of the story. Decide as a class how long team recordings should be.

- If you choose to do this, you must first break the story down into its major parts and make up a script to include the various parts for which each of you will be responsible.

- Next, work independently to write your script and practice your own part.

- Meet with the rest of your group and rehearse your summary. Time it on your tape.

- Get feedback from another group on what should be added to or deleted from your tape. Remember to write it as though the listener does not know the story plot. You must, therefore, include everything necessary to make it understandable.

- Now that you have considered other opinions and modified your dialogue, work on your final recording.

Another way to approach this is to simply take the scene from the diorama and act it out on tape. For example, maybe you chose the part where Boone and Little Bear became "blood brothers." Find that section of the book and rewrite it to fit your team's needs. Each member of your team could play a part.

- Assign a narrator to tell what has happened up to this point in the story. (5- 10 minute script)

- Decide which members of the team will dramatize the parts of the characters you have chosen. Practice their voices. When you are ready, record the manuscript.

- After you have practiced and recorded your script, have another team listen to it and make suggestions on additions or deletions that they think might be necessary to better understand the story. Edit your script and make your final recording.

- Once you have your recording finished, your group is ready to present it, along with the diorama, to the entire class.

A Look Into The Past

For this cooperative group activity, you will be writing in teams of two to four.

Imagine that Mr. Johnson finally recovered his composure and contacted an official connected with England's Prime Minister. He informed this official of what he had just seen and suggested that the British Secret Service might be interested in this magic cupboard. All that was necessary to find out about the past, or perhaps, to change the past, would be to place an historic figure or item into the cupboard and it would come to life. Which individuals might the Prime Minister or members of his staff want to interview and why? What items from history might they find of significance and importance today? In the chart below, write the names of the people or items in which the Prime Minister and staff would be interested. In each case, include the reasons for their interest. A few examples have been provided for you.

Item	Reason
Roman catapult	For historians to study early warfare
Chinese gunpowder	For possible use before Europe was introduced to it

People	Reason
William the Conqueror	To find out about the Battle of Hastings
King Henry VIII	Why he separated from the church

A Look Into The Past *(cont.)*

For this activity present four historical events from any country and recall some of the significant figures who were most responsible for those events. Write down next to the event the pertinent details of what actually happened and do research for accuracy of information. Then in the next column, change the results in one of two ways: the event never happened; the outcome should be changed in some way.

Event	*New Outcome*
Example: **The Lincoln Assassination** Lincoln was assassinated while attending a performance at Ford's Theater in Washington, D.C. Under the new president's leadership, the South was treated more harshly.	If Mr. Lincoln did not attend the theater that night, the assassination might have been prevented. The result might have been a more sympathetic handling of the ravaged South.
1.	
2.	
3.	
4.	

Unit Test

Matching: Match these quotes with the characters who said them.

Boone	Patrick	Little Bear	Omri	Mr. Johnson
Gillon	mother	father	Tommy	

1 _____ " 'That was the key to my grandmother's jewel box, that she got from Florence.' "

2. _____ " 'Well I'll be jiggered! A bloomin' Indian! ' "

3. _____ " 'Omri, have you been in the greenhouse lately?' "

4. _____ " 'Don't you touch him! I bought him, I changed him-he's mine!' "

5. _____ " 'Ah ain't aimin' to drink no more o' that as lawng as Ah live!' "

True or False: Write true or false next to each statement below.

1. _____ Omri only shares his secret with Patrick.

2. _____ Boone and Little Bear fight throughout the story and never resolve their differences.

3. _____ Little Bear and his demands did not concern or upset Omri.

4. _____ Boone and Little Bear were quite content with their new life in England.

5. _____ Omri refused to have a wedding feast for Little Bear and Bright Stars as ordered by Little Bear.

Short Answer: Provide a short answer for each of these questions.

1. Why did Adiel hide the cupboard? _____

_____

2. Why did Little Bear shoot Boone with his bow and arrow? _____

_____

3 What did friendship mean to Omri? _____

_____

4. Why did Omri get so upset with the way Patrick treated the men? _____

_____

5. Why did the boys finally send Little Bear and Boone back? _____

_____

Essay: Answer these essay questions on the back of this paper.

1. Would you characterize Omri as a sensitive or insensitive boy? Justify your answer with examples from the story.

2. Which do you think had the magic, the cupboard or the key? Choose one and support your answer.

Response

Explain the meaning of each of these quotations from *The Indian in the Cupboard.*

Chapter 1 :   *"Most of the keys were much too big, but there were half a dozen that were about the right size. All but one of these were very ordinary."*

Chapter 1:   *"Omri put the cupboard on his bedside table, and opening it, looked inside thoughtfully. What would he put in it?"*

Chapter 2:   *Omri tells Patrick at school, "Your present was the best thing I got."*

Chapter 2:   *" 'Not want toy,' said the Indian, and turned his back, folding both arms across his chest with an air of finality."*

Chapter 3:   *"Not only was his Indian no mere toy come to life, he was a real person, somehow magicked out of the past of over two hundred years ago."*

Chapter 4:   *"The horse's speed was remarkable, but Omri found that by running along the lawn beside the path he could keep up quite easily."*

Chapter 5:   *" 'Well I'll be jiggered!' he breathed. 'A bloomin' Indian!' "*

Chapter 6:   *"The old man gazed up at him, blankly at first, and then with a dawning terror."*

Chapter 7:   *" 'I've been to Yapp's,' said Patrick. 'I bought you something.' "*

Chapter 8:   *"He burst in through the door and saw exactly what he'd dreaded—Patrick, bent over the cupboard, just turning the key to open it."*

Chapter 9:   *"Suddenly some tiny thing whizzed past Omri's ear and struck the crate beside him with a ping!"*

Chapter 10:   *"Little Bear finished his breakfast and stood up. 'Now we fight.' "*

Chapter 11:   *"Little Bear got really sick and tired of being imprisoned, and started to take drastic action."*

Chapter 12:   *"Without stopping to think, Omri hurled himself against the door, kicking and banging his fists."*

Chapter 13:   *" 'Kin Ah draw a mite on yer paper?' he asked."*

Chapter 14:   *"He looked back at Boone swiftly, and his blood froze. The cowboy had an arrow sticking out of his chest."*

Chapter 15:   *"There was something else in his hand-something cold and knobbly, twice as heavy as Little Bear. He opened his fingers and both boys leaned over to look."*

Chapter 16:   *"Out crept a beautiful Indian girl. There was enough light in the room now for Omri to see the black of her hair, the chestnut brown of her skin, the bright red of her dress."*

Chapter 16:   *"Bright Stars bound their wrists together with a strip of hide torn from the hem of her red dress."*

Chapter 16:   *"Omri put his group—the Indian, the girl, and the horse-on the shelf nearest his bed where he could see it easily. He laid the beaded belt—still real—beside it."*

Teacher Note: Choose an appropriate number of quotes for your students.

Conversations

Work in size-appropriate groups to write and perform the conversations that might have occurred in each of the following situations.

- Omri's mother tells her husband the real power of the key that Omri selected for the cupboard. Relate his reactions to this. (2 people)

- Patrick and another friend talk about the change in Omri's behavior when he refuses to skateboard with them, and prefers to play with the plastic Indian. (2 people)

- The Indian tells the chief that some form of magic took him away into a giant's land the previous night. (2 people)

- Omri tells the secret to his mother. She in turn tells Omri her childhood secret of the key. (2 people)

- Omri's parents discuss whether or not they should let Omri continue amusing himself with his little friend. (2 people)

- Omri finally shares his secret about Little Bear with his brothers, Adiel and Gillon. (3 people)

- Gillon and two friends discuss how to use the cupboard to find out the causes of World War II by bringing back the main participants to life for an interview. (3 people)

- Omri's gardener tells a neighbor about seeing Omri and tiny people with horses running through his garden. (2 people)

- Tommy returns to the front in World War I and reports to his senior officers about some secret weapon that transported him through time. (3 people)

- Gillon tells the secret of the cupboard to some friends and suggests that they place plastic space models in the cupboard as part of their science project to learn about space travel. (4 people)

- Omri tells his parents on Gillon for not respecting his property and "using" real people for his reports at school. (4 people)

- Patrick gives Boone advice on how to stop crying all the time. (2 people)

- April and a friend tell the teacher about the secret things passed between Patrick and Omri. (3 people)

- Patrick tells all to Mr. Johnson and Mrs. Hunt and shows them Boone. (3 people)

- Mr. Johnson and Mrs. Hunt decide what is to be done about the boys now that they have sent them back to class. (2 people)

- The art teacher and an expert from the Art Institute discuss the remarkable drawing and how it might have been made. (2 people)

- April and three friends discuss Patrick's and Omri's strange behavior of the last few days. They decide to spy on Omri's room which is within telescope range of April's house. (4 people)

- Mr. Yapp, knowing the two figures are alive, calls a scientist friend to discuss this great discovery, and how they can use it to their advantage. (2 people)

- Boone and Little Bear discuss their futures while prisoners in Omri's pocket. (2 people)

Bibliography

Fiction

Adams, Richard. *Watership Down.* (Macmillan, 1974)

Adler, Carole S. *Good-bye Pink Pig.* (Putnam, 1985)

Alcock, Vivien. *The Stonewalkers.* (Delacorte, 1983)

Ames, Mildred. *Is There Life on a Plastic Planet?* (Dutton, 1975)

Auch, Mary Jane. *The Witching of Ben Wagner.* (Houghton Mifflin, 1987)

Babbitt, Natalie. *The Search for Delicious.* (Farrar, 1969)

Banks, Lynne Reid. *The Return of the Indian in the Cupboard.* (Doubleday, 1986)

Beachcroft, Nina. *The Wishing People.* (Dutton, 1982)

Bellairs, John. *The Figure in the Shadows.* (Dial, 1975)

Branscum, Robbie. *The Adventures of Johnny May.* (Harper, 1984)

Byars, Betsy. *The Blossoms and the Green Phantom.* (Delacort, 1987)

Canfield, Dorothy. *Understood Betsy.* (Buccaneer, 1946)

Cresswell, Helen. *Moondial.* (Macmillan, 1987)

Dunlop, Eileen. *The Maze Stone.* (Putnam, 1983)

Enright, Elizabeth. *Thimble Summer.* (Henry Holt, 1976)

Houghton, Eric. *Steps Out of Time.* (Lothrop, 1980)

Steele, Mary Q. *Journey Outside.* (Penguin, 1969)

Steele, Mary Q. *The True Men.* (Greenwillow, 1976)

Winthrop, Elizabeth. *The Castle in the Attic.* (Bantam, 1985)

Native Americans of North America—Fiction

Armer, Laura A. *Waterless Mountain.* (McKay, 1932)

Crompton, Anne Eliot. *The Ice Trail,* (Routledge, 1980)

Goble, Paul. *Lone Bull's Horse Raid.* (Bradbury, 1973)

Richter, Conrad. *Light in the Forest.* (Bantom, 1966)

Native Americans of North America—Non Fiction

Behrens, June. *Powwow.* (Childrens Press, 1983)

Fichter, George S. *How the Plains Indian Lived.* (McKay, 1980)

Glass, Paul. *Songs and Stories of the North American Indian.* (Grosset & Dunlap, 1970)

Hofsinde, Robert (Graywolf). *Indian Arts.* (William Morrow and Company, 1971)

Morris, Richard B. *The Indian Wars.* (Lerner, 1985)

Sheppard, Sally. *Indians of the Plains.* (Franklin Watts, 1976)

Siegel, Beatrice. *The Indians of the Woodland, before and after the Pilgrims.* (Walker, 1972)

Native American Legends

Bierhorst, John. *Doctor Coyote: A Native American Aesop's Fables.* (MacMillan, 1987)

Caduto, Michael J. & Bruchac, Joseph. *Keepers of the Earth: Native American Stories and Environmental Activities for Children.* (Fulcrum, Inc., 1988)

dePaola, Tomie. *The Legend of Bluebonnet.* (G.P. Putnam's Sons, 1983)

Goble, Paul. *Star Boy.* (Bradbury Press, 1983)

Answer Key

Page 10

1. Accept appropriate responses.
2. Omri tries not to show his disappointment.
3. He will be able to store his things in it and he loves cupboards.
4. It belonged to her mother's leather jewel box.
5. There is an Indian in his cupboard.
6. He feels the others might laugh at him if the Indian disappears while he is gone. Also, he wants to keep it to himself, at first.
7. He doesn't laugh because the Indian is so brave.
8. Little Bear thinks that the tepee is a toy. In addition, his people do not use tepees.
9. They could turn plastic items into real things.
10. He belongs to the Iroquois Tribe.

Page 15

1. Accept appropriate responses.
2. His horse kicks Little Bear in the leg.
3. He finds a British World War I medic.
4. He thinks that he is needed there.
5. Omri gives him a knight's battle ax.
6. He builds a long house.
7. He learns that it was introduced by the French and English.
8. He has to get a bow and arrows for Little Bear.
9. He makes his tepee and sews it up.
10. He becomes frightened and dies.

Page 20

1. Accept appropriate answers.
2. Omri buys him a new seed tray, and maize and marrow seeds.
3. Patrick buys Omri a cowboy and a horse.
4. He thinks a little ball of tar would burn for a long time.
5. He is creating his own human toy.
6. Patrick threatens to tell the secret.
7. The horse kicks a large knot-hole out of the crate.
8. Boone thinks this because he was drunk the night before.
9. Little Bear will do a dance if Omri brings him a wife.
10. Boone's friends call him "Boohoo" Boone because he cries all the time.

Page 25

1. Accept appropriate responses.
2. Little Bear calls Omri this because Omri cooks food for him.
3. They have to call a truce.
4. Little Bear gets up and challenges Boone to a fight.
5. Boone says to forget it since they have never been washed.
6. The suggestion is that they might never get home again.
7. They get kicked out because Little Bear keeps stabbing Omri in the leg causing him to cry out. This creates a disturbance.
8. Patrick is knocked to the floor. This could have killed the two little men.
9. He realizes that Patrick just uses the men and does not view them as real.
10. The headmaster's face is white because he sees the little men and he is probably in shock.

Answer Key *(cont.)*

Page 30

1. Accept appropriate responses.
2. Patrick confesses so the headmaster will forget about calling his father.
3. Omri tells Patrick that they are not safe with him.
4. He insists on having a wife.
5. Boone is an artist.
6. Patrick defends Omri at Mr. Yapp's when he is accused of theft.
7. They realize that they might be in the giant world forever.
8. Little Bear shoots Boone near the heart.
9. Little Bear risks his life and finds the key.
10. They leave it empty just in case they decide to call their little men back to check on things.

Pages 38-41

Create a display of these culminating activities for the bulletin board or shelf.

Page 42

Matching

1) Omri's mother 2) Tommy 3) Omri's father 4) Patrick 5) Boone

True or False

1. True
2. False; they become blood brothers.
3. False; Omri was finding it increasingly difficult to meet Little Bear's demands.
4. False; they wanted to return to their homes.
5. True

Short Answer

1. Adiel hid the cupboard because he thought Omri hid his shorts.
2. Boone was shot because Little Bear didn't like Boone cheering as the television cowboys were killing the Indians.
3. Friendship was very important to Omri. It meant companionship, trust, and selflessness.
4. Omri was upset because instead of treating the men with dignity, Patrick used them.
5. The boys sent the people back because each had a life of his/her own to live. They were real people.

Essay

1. Accept appropriate responses. These should include Omri's concern for the characters as real people.
2. Accept appropriate responses. The student's argument should be developed logically with support clearly explained.

Page 43

Accept all reasonable and well-supported answers.

Page 44

Perform the conversations in class. Ask students to respond to the conversations in several different ways, such as, "Are the conversations realistic?" or, "Are the words the characters say in line with their personalities?"

The Indian in the Cupboard Pattern. See page 5 for suggested uses.

48